In Loving Memory of

_____

_____

Date of Birth

_____

Laid to Rest

In Loving Memory
Please Sign In

Name _____ Relationship _____

Address _____ Email _____

Memory
or Note _____

Name _____ Relationship _____

Address _____ Email _____

Memory
or Note _____

Name _____ Relationship _____

Address _____ Email _____

Memory
or Note _____

Name _____ Relationship _____

Address _____ Email _____

Memory
or Note _____

Name _____ Relationship _____

Address _____ Email _____

Memory
or Note _____

In Loving Memory

Please Sign In

Name _____ *Relationship* _____

Address _____ *Email* _____

Memory
or Note _____

_____

Name _____ *Relationship* _____

Address _____ *Email* _____

Memory
or Note _____

_____

Name _____ *Relationship* _____

Address _____ *Email* _____

Memory
or Note _____

_____

Name _____ *Relationship* _____

Address _____ *Email* _____

Memory
or Note _____

_____

Name _____ *Relationship* _____

Address _____ *Email* _____

Memory
or Note _____

_____

In Loving Memory

Please Sign In

Name _____ *Relationship* _____

Address _____ *Email* _____

Memory
or Note _____

Name _____ *Relationship* _____

Address _____ *Email* _____

Memory
or Note _____

Name _____ *Relationship* _____

Address _____ *Email* _____

Memory
or Note _____

Name _____ *Relationship* _____

Address _____ *Email* _____

Memory
or Note _____

Name _____ *Relationship* _____

Address _____ *Email* _____

Memory
or Note _____

In Loving Memory
Please Sign In

Name _____ *Relationship* _____

Address _____ *Email* _____

Memory
or Note _____
_____

Name _____ *Relationship* _____

Address _____ *Email* _____

Memory
or Note _____
_____

Name _____ *Relationship* _____

Address _____ *Email* _____

Memory
or Note _____
_____

Name _____ *Relationship* _____

Address _____ *Email* _____

Memory
or Note _____
_____

Name _____ *Relationship* _____

Address _____ *Email* _____

Memory
or Note _____
_____

In Loving Memory

Please Sign In

Name _____ *Relationship* _____

Address _____ *Email* _____

Memory
or Note _____

_____

Name _____ *Relationship* _____

Address _____ *Email* _____

Memory
or Note _____

_____

Name _____ *Relationship* _____

Address _____ *Email* _____

Memory
or Note _____

_____

Name _____ *Relationship* _____

Address _____ *Email* _____

Memory
or Note _____

_____

Name _____ *Relationship* _____

Address _____ *Email* _____

Memory
or Note _____

_____

In Loving Memory
Please Sign In

Name _____ *Relationship* _____

Address _____ *Email* _____

Memory or Note _____

Name _____ *Relationship* _____

Address _____ *Email* _____

Memory or Note _____

Name _____ *Relationship* _____

Address _____ *Email* _____

Memory or Note _____

Name _____ *Relationship* _____

Address _____ *Email* _____

Memory or Note _____

Name _____ *Relationship* _____

Address _____ *Email* _____

Memory or Note _____

In Loving Memory

Please Sign In

Name _____ *Relationship* _____

Address _____ *Email* _____

Memory or Note _____

Name _____ *Relationship* _____

Address _____ *Email* _____

Memory or Note _____

Name _____ *Relationship* _____

Address _____ *Email* _____

Memory or Note _____

Name _____ *Relationship* _____

Address _____ *Email* _____

Memory or Note _____

Name _____ *Relationship* _____

Address _____ *Email* _____

Memory or Note _____

In Loving Memory
Please Sign In

Name _____ Relationship _____

Address _____ Email _____

Memory
or Note _____

Name _____ Relationship _____

Address _____ Email _____

Memory
or Note _____

Name _____ Relationship _____

Address _____ Email _____

Memory
or Note _____

Name _____ Relationship _____

Address _____ Email _____

Memory
or Note _____

Name _____ Relationship _____

Address _____ Email _____

Memory
or Note _____

In Loving Memory

Please Sign In

Name _____ *Relationship* _____
Address _____ *Email* _____
Memory
or Note _____

_____

Name _____ *Relationship* _____
Address _____ *Email* _____
Memory
or Note _____

_____

Name _____ *Relationship* _____
Address _____ *Email* _____
Memory
or Note _____

_____

Name _____ *Relationship* _____
Address _____ *Email* _____
Memory
or Note _____

_____

Name _____ *Relationship* _____
Address _____ *Email* _____
Memory
or Note _____

_____

In Loving Memory
Please Sign In

Name _____   *Relationship* _____

Address _____   *Email* _____

Memory or Note _____

Name _____   *Relationship* _____

Address _____   *Email* _____

Memory or Note _____

Name _____   *Relationship* _____

Address _____   *Email* _____

Memory or Note _____

Name _____   *Relationship* _____

Address _____   *Email* _____

Memory or Note _____

Name _____   *Relationship* _____

Address _____   *Email* _____

Memory or Note _____

In Loving Memory

Please Sign In

Name _____   Relationship _____

Address _____   Email _____

Memory _____
or Note _____

Name _____   Relationship _____

Address _____   Email _____

Memory _____
or Note _____

Name _____   Relationship _____

Address _____   Email _____

Memory _____
or Note _____

Name _____   Relationship _____

Address _____   Email _____

Memory _____
or Note _____

Name _____   Relationship _____

Address _____   Email _____

Memory _____
or Note _____

In Loving Memory
Please Sign In

Name _____ *Relationship* _____

Address _____ *Email* _____

Memory or Note _____

Name _____ *Relationship* _____

Address _____ *Email* _____

Memory or Note _____

Name _____ *Relationship* _____

Address _____ *Email* _____

Memory or Note _____

Name _____ *Relationship* _____

Address _____ *Email* _____

Memory or Note _____

Name _____ *Relationship* _____

Address _____ *Email* _____

Memory or Note _____

In Loving Memory

Please Sign In

Name _____ *Relationship* _____
Address _____ *Email* _____
Memory
or Note _____

Name _____ *Relationship* _____
Address _____ *Email* _____
Memory
or Note _____

Name _____ *Relationship* _____
Address _____ *Email* _____
Memory
or Note _____

Name _____ *Relationship* _____
Address _____ *Email* _____
Memory
or Note _____

Name _____ *Relationship* _____
Address _____ *Email* _____
Memory
or Note _____

In Loving Memory
Please Sign In

Name _____ *Relationship* _____

Address _____ *Email* _____

Memory
or Note _____

Name _____ *Relationship* _____

Address _____ *Email* _____

Memory
or Note _____

Name _____ *Relationship* _____

Address _____ *Email* _____

Memory
or Note _____

Name _____ *Relationship* _____

Address _____ *Email* _____

Memory
or Note _____

Name _____ *Relationship* _____

Address _____ *Email* _____

Memory
or Note _____

In Loving Memory

Please Sign In

Name _____ *Relationship* _____

Address _____ *Email* _____

Memory
or Note _____

_____

Name _____ *Relationship* _____

Address _____ *Email* _____

Memory
or Note _____

_____

Name _____ *Relationship* _____

Address _____ *Email* _____

Memory
or Note _____

_____

Name _____ *Relationship* _____

Address _____ *Email* _____

Memory
or Note _____

_____

Name _____ *Relationship* _____

Address _____ *Email* _____

Memory
or Note _____

_____

In Loving Memory

Please Sign In

Name _____   *Relationship* _____
Address _____   *Email* _____
Memory
or Note _____

Name _____   *Relationship* _____
Address _____   *Email* _____
Memory
or Note _____

Name _____   *Relationship* _____
Address _____   *Email* _____
Memory
or Note _____

Name _____   *Relationship* _____
Address _____   *Email* _____
Memory
or Note _____

Name _____   *Relationship* _____
Address _____   *Email* _____
Memory
or Note _____

In Loving Memory

Please Sign In

Name _____   *Relationship* _____

Address _____   *Email* _____

Memory
or Note _____

_____

Name _____   *Relationship* _____

Address _____   *Email* _____

Memory
or Note _____

_____

Name _____   *Relationship* _____

Address _____   *Email* _____

Memory
or Note _____

_____

Name _____   *Relationship* _____

Address _____   *Email* _____

Memory
or Note _____

_____

Name _____   *Relationship* _____

Address _____   *Email* _____

Memory
or Note _____

_____

In Loving Memory

Please Sign In

Name _____ *Relationship* _____

Address _____ *Email* _____

Memory or Note _____

_____

Name _____ *Relationship* _____

Address _____ *Email* _____

Memory or Note _____

_____

Name _____ *Relationship* _____

Address _____ *Email* _____

Memory or Note _____

_____

Name _____ *Relationship* _____

Address _____ *Email* _____

Memory or Note _____

_____

Name _____ *Relationship* _____

Address _____ *Email* _____

Memory or Note _____

_____

In Loving Memory

Please Sign In

Name _____ *Relationship* _____
Address _____ *Email* _____
Memory or Note _____

Name _____ *Relationship* _____
Address _____ *Email* _____
Memory or Note _____

Name _____ *Relationship* _____
Address _____ *Email* _____
Memory or Note _____

Name _____ *Relationship* _____
Address _____ *Email* _____
Memory or Note _____

Name _____ *Relationship* _____
Address _____ *Email* _____
Memory or Note _____

In Loving Memory

Please Sign In

Name _____ *Relationship* _____
Address _____ *Email* _____
Memory
or Note _____

Name _____ *Relationship* _____
Address _____ *Email* _____
Memory
or Note _____

Name _____ *Relationship* _____
Address _____ *Email* _____
Memory
or Note _____

Name _____ *Relationship* _____
Address _____ *Email* _____
Memory
or Note _____

Name _____ *Relationship* _____
Address _____ *Email* _____
Memory
or Note _____

In Loving Memory
Please Sign In

Name _____   *Relationship* _____

Address _____   *Email* _____

Memory or Note _____

_____

Name _____   *Relationship* _____

Address _____   *Email* _____

Memory or Note _____

_____

Name _____   *Relationship* _____

Address _____   *Email* _____

Memory or Note _____

_____

Name _____   *Relationship* _____

Address _____   *Email* _____

Memory or Note _____

_____

Name _____   *Relationship* _____

Address _____   *Email* _____

Memory or Note _____

In Loving Memory
Please Sign In

Name _____ *Relationship* _____

Address _____ *Email* _____

Memory
or Note _____

Name _____ *Relationship* _____

Address _____ *Email* _____

Memory
or Note _____

Name _____ *Relationship* _____

Address _____ *Email* _____

Memory
or Note _____

Name _____ *Relationship* _____

Address _____ *Email* _____

Memory
or Note _____

Name _____ *Relationship* _____

Address _____ *Email* _____

Memory
or Note _____

In Loving Memory
Please Sign In

Name _____   *Relationship* _____
Address _____   *Email* _____
Memory
or Note _____
_____

Name _____   *Relationship* _____
Address _____   *Email* _____
Memory
or Note _____
_____

Name _____   *Relationship* _____
Address _____   *Email* _____
Memory
or Note _____
_____

Name _____   *Relationship* _____
Address _____   *Email* _____
Memory
or Note _____
_____

Name _____   *Relationship* _____
Address _____   *Email* _____
Memory
or Note _____
_____

In Loving Memory
Please Sign In

Name _____ *Relationship* _____

Address _____ *Email* _____

Memory or Note _____

Name _____ *Relationship* _____

Address _____ *Email* _____

Memory or Note _____

Name _____ *Relationship* _____

Address _____ *Email* _____

Memory or Note _____

Name _____ *Relationship* _____

Address _____ *Email* _____

Memory or Note _____

Name _____ *Relationship* _____

Address _____ *Email* _____

Memory or Note _____

In Loving Memory

Please Sign In

Name _____ *Relationship* _____

Address _____ *Email* _____

Memory or Note _____

Name _____ *Relationship* _____

Address _____ *Email* _____

Memory or Note _____

Name _____ *Relationship* _____

Address _____ *Email* _____

Memory or Note _____

Name _____ *Relationship* _____

Address _____ *Email* _____

Memory or Note _____

Name _____ *Relationship* _____

Address _____ *Email* _____

Memory or Note _____

In Loving Memory
Please Sign In

Name _____   *Relationship* _____

Address _____   *Email* _____

Memory
or Note _____

Name _____   *Relationship* _____

Address _____   *Email* _____

Memory
or Note _____

Name _____   *Relationship* _____

Address _____   *Email* _____

Memory
or Note _____

Name _____   *Relationship* _____

Address _____   *Email* _____

Memory
or Note _____

Name _____   *Relationship* _____

Address _____   *Email* _____

Memory
or Note _____

In Loving Memory
Please Sign In

Name _____   *Relationship* _____
Address _____   *Email* _____
Memory
or Note _____

Name _____   *Relationship* _____
Address _____   *Email* _____
Memory
or Note _____

Name _____   *Relationship* _____
Address _____   *Email* _____
Memory
or Note _____

Name _____   *Relationship* _____
Address _____   *Email* _____
Memory
or Note _____

Name _____   *Relationship* _____
Address _____   *Email* _____
Memory
or Note _____

In Loving Memory
Please Sign In

Name _____ *Relationship* _____

Address _____ *Email* _____

Memory
or Note _____

Name _____ *Relationship* _____

Address _____ *Email* _____

Memory
or Note _____

Name _____ *Relationship* _____

Address _____ *Email* _____

Memory
or Note _____

Name _____ *Relationship* _____

Address _____ *Email* _____

Memory
or Note _____

Name _____ *Relationship* _____

Address _____ *Email* _____

Memory
or Note _____

In Loving Memory
Please Sign In

Name _____ *Relationship* _____

Address _____ *Email* _____

Memory
or Note _____

Name _____ *Relationship* _____

Address _____ *Email* _____

Memory
or Note _____

Name _____ *Relationship* _____

Address _____ *Email* _____

Memory
or Note _____

Name _____ *Relationship* _____

Address _____ *Email* _____

Memory
or Note _____

Name _____ *Relationship* _____

Address _____ *Email* _____

Memory
or Note _____

In Loving Memory

Please Sign In

Name _____ *Relationship* _____

Address _____ *Email* _____

Memory
or Note _____

_____

Name _____ *Relationship* _____

Address _____ *Email* _____

Memory
or Note _____

_____

Name _____ *Relationship* _____

Address _____ *Email* _____

Memory
or Note _____

_____

Name _____ *Relationship* _____

Address _____ *Email* _____

Memory
or Note _____

_____

Name _____ *Relationship* _____

Address _____ *Email* _____

Memory
or Note _____

_____

In Loving Memory

Name _____ *Relationship* _____

Address _____ *Email* _____

Memory
or Note _____
_____

Name _____ *Relationship* _____

Address _____ *Email* _____

Memory
or Note _____
_____

Name _____ *Relationship* _____

Address _____ *Email* _____

Memory
or Note _____
_____

Name _____ *Relationship* _____

Address _____ *Email* _____

Memory
or Note _____
_____

Name _____ *Relationship* _____

Address _____ *Email* _____

Memory
or Note _____
_____

In Loving Memory
Please Sign In

Name _____ *Relationship* _____

Address _____ *Email* _____

*Memory
or Note* _____
_____

Name _____ *Relationship* _____

Address _____ *Email* _____

*Memory
or Note* _____
_____

Name _____ *Relationship* _____

Address _____ *Email* _____

*Memory
or Note* _____
_____

Name _____ *Relationship* _____

Address _____ *Email* _____

*Memory
or Note* _____
_____

Name _____ *Relationship* _____

Address _____ *Email* _____

*Memory
or Note* _____
_____

In Loving Memory

Please Sign In

Name _____   *Relationship* _____

Address _____   *Email* _____

Memory
or Note _____

_____

Name _____   *Relationship* _____

Address _____   *Email* _____

Memory
or Note _____

_____

Name _____   *Relationship* _____

Address _____   *Email* _____

Memory
or Note _____

_____

Name _____   *Relationship* _____

Address _____   *Email* _____

Memory
or Note _____

_____

Name _____   *Relationship* _____

Address _____   *Email* _____

Memory
or Note _____

_____

In Loving Memory

Please Sign In

Name _____ *Relationship* _____

Address _____ *Email* _____

Memory or Note _____

Name _____ *Relationship* _____

Address _____ *Email* _____

Memory or Note _____

Name _____ *Relationship* _____

Address _____ *Email* _____

Memory or Note _____

Name _____ *Relationship* _____

Address _____ *Email* _____

Memory or Note _____

Name _____ *Relationship* _____

Address _____ *Email* _____

Memory or Note _____

In Loving Memory

Please Sign In

Name _____ *Relationship* _____
Address _____ *Email* _____
Memory
or Note _____

Name _____ *Relationship* _____
Address _____ *Email* _____
Memory
or Note _____

Name _____ *Relationship* _____
Address _____ *Email* _____
Memory
or Note _____

Name _____ *Relationship* _____
Address _____ *Email* _____
Memory
or Note _____

Name _____ *Relationship* _____
Address _____ *Email* _____
Memory
or Note _____

In Loving Memory

Please Sign In

Name _____ *Relationship* _____

Address _____ *Email* _____

Memory
or Note _____

Name _____ *Relationship* _____

Address _____ *Email* _____

Memory
or Note _____

Name _____ *Relationship* _____

Address _____ *Email* _____

Memory
or Note _____

Name _____ *Relationship* _____

Address _____ *Email* _____

Memory
or Note _____

Name _____ *Relationship* _____

Address _____ *Email* _____

Memory
or Note _____

In Loving Memory

Please Sign In

Name _____   *Relationship* _____
Address _____   *Email* _____
Memory or Note _____

Name _____   *Relationship* _____
Address _____   *Email* _____
Memory or Note _____

Name _____   *Relationship* _____
Address _____   *Email* _____
Memory or Note _____

Name _____   *Relationship* _____
Address _____   *Email* _____
Memory or Note _____

Name _____   *Relationship* _____
Address _____   *Email* _____
Memory or Note _____

In Loving Memory

Please Sign In

Name _____   *Relationship* _____
Address _____   *Email* _____
Memory
or Note _____

Name _____   *Relationship* _____
Address _____   *Email* _____
Memory
or Note _____

Name _____   *Relationship* _____
Address _____   *Email* _____
Memory
or Note _____

Name _____   *Relationship* _____
Address _____   *Email* _____
Memory
or Note _____

Name _____   *Relationship* _____
Address _____   *Email* _____
Memory
or Note _____

In Loving Memory

Please Sign In

Name _____ *Relationship* _____

Address _____ *Email* _____

Memory _____
or Note _____

Name _____ *Relationship* _____

Address _____ *Email* _____

Memory _____
or Note _____

Name _____ *Relationship* _____

Address _____ *Email* _____

Memory _____
or Note _____

Name _____ *Relationship* _____

Address _____ *Email* _____

Memory _____
or Note _____

Name _____ *Relationship* _____

Address _____ *Email* _____

Memory _____
or Note _____

In Loving Memory
Please Sign In

Name _____ *Relationship* _____

Address _____ *Email* _____

Memory or Note _____

Name _____ *Relationship* _____

Address _____ *Email* _____

Memory or Note _____

Name _____ *Relationship* _____

Address _____ *Email* _____

Memory or Note _____

Name _____ *Relationship* _____

Address _____ *Email* _____

Memory or Note _____

Name _____ *Relationship* _____

Address _____ *Email* _____

Memory or Note _____

In Loving Memory

Please Sign In

Name _____ *Relationship* _____

Address _____ *Email* _____

Memory or Note _____

Name _____ *Relationship* _____

Address _____ *Email* _____

Memory or Note _____

Name _____ *Relationship* _____

Address _____ *Email* _____

Memory or Note _____

Name _____ *Relationship* _____

Address _____ *Email* _____

Memory or Note _____

Name _____ *Relationship* _____

Address _____ *Email* _____

Memory or Note _____

In Loving Memory

Please Sign In

Name _____ *Relationship* _____

Address _____ *Email* _____

Memory
or Note _____

_____

Name _____ *Relationship* _____

Address _____ *Email* _____

Memory
or Note _____

_____

Name _____ *Relationship* _____

Address _____ *Email* _____

Memory
or Note _____

_____

Name _____ *Relationship* _____

Address _____ *Email* _____

Memory
or Note _____

_____

Name _____ *Relationship* _____

Address _____ *Email* _____

Memory
or Note _____

_____

In Loving Memory

Please Sign In

Name _____   *Relationship* _____

Address _____   *Email* _____

Memory or Note _____

Name _____   *Relationship* _____

Address _____   *Email* _____

Memory or Note _____

Name _____   *Relationship* _____

Address _____   *Email* _____

Memory or Note _____

Name _____   *Relationship* _____

Address _____   *Email* _____

Memory or Note _____

Name _____   *Relationship* _____

Address _____   *Email* _____

Memory or Note _____

In Loving Memory

Please Sign In

Name _____   *Relationship* _____

Address _____   *Email* _____

Memory
or Note _____

Name _____   *Relationship* _____

Address _____   *Email* _____

Memory
or Note _____

Name _____   *Relationship* _____

Address _____   *Email* _____

Memory
or Note _____

Name _____   *Relationship* _____

Address _____   *Email* _____

Memory
or Note _____

Name _____   *Relationship* _____

Address _____   *Email* _____

Memory
or Note _____

In Loving Memory

Please Sign In

Name _____ *Relationship* _____

Address _____ *Email* _____

Memory _____
or Note _____

Name _____ *Relationship* _____

Address _____ *Email* _____

Memory _____
or Note _____

Name _____ *Relationship* _____

Address _____ *Email* _____

Memory _____
or Note _____

Name _____ *Relationship* _____

Address _____ *Email* _____

Memory _____
or Note _____

Name _____ *Relationship* _____

Address _____ *Email* _____

Memory _____
or Note _____

In Loving Memory
Please Sign In

Name _____ *Relationship* _____

Address _____ *Email* _____

Memory _____
or Note _____

Name _____ *Relationship* _____

Address _____ *Email* _____

Memory _____
or Note _____

Name _____ *Relationship* _____

Address _____ *Email* _____

Memory _____
or Note _____

Name _____ *Relationship* _____

Address _____ *Email* _____

Memory _____
or Note _____

Name _____ *Relationship* _____

Address _____ *Email* _____

Memory _____
or Note _____

In Loving Memory
Please Sign In

Name _____ *Relationship* _____

Address _____ *Email* _____

Memory
or Note _____

Name _____ *Relationship* _____

Address _____ *Email* _____

Memory
or Note _____

Name _____ *Relationship* _____

Address _____ *Email* _____

Memory
or Note _____

Name _____ *Relationship* _____

Address _____ *Email* _____

Memory
or Note _____

Name _____ *Relationship* _____

Address _____ *Email* _____

Memory
or Note _____

In Loving Memory

Please Sign In

Name _____   *Relationship* _____

Address _____   *Email* _____

Memory
or Note _____
_____

Name _____   *Relationship* _____

Address _____   *Email* _____

Memory
or Note _____
_____

Name _____   *Relationship* _____

Address _____   *Email* _____

Memory
or Note _____
_____

Name _____   *Relationship* _____

Address _____   *Email* _____

Memory
or Note _____
_____

Name _____   *Relationship* _____

Address _____   *Email* _____

Memory
or Note _____
_____

In Loving Memory

Please Sign In

Name _____ *Relationship* _____
Address _____ *Email* _____
Memory
or Note _____

Name _____ *Relationship* _____
Address _____ *Email* _____
Memory
or Note _____

Name _____ *Relationship* _____
Address _____ *Email* _____
Memory
or Note _____

Name _____ *Relationship* _____
Address _____ *Email* _____
Memory
or Note _____

Name _____ *Relationship* _____
Address _____ *Email* _____
Memory
or Note _____

In Loving Memory
Please Sign In

Name _____ *Relationship* _____

Address _____ *Email* _____

Memory or Note _____

Name _____ *Relationship* _____

Address _____ *Email* _____

Memory or Note _____

Name _____ *Relationship* _____

Address _____ *Email* _____

Memory or Note _____

Name _____ *Relationship* _____

Address _____ *Email* _____

Memory or Note _____

Name _____ *Relationship* _____

Address _____ *Email* _____

Memory or Note _____

Gift Log

Flowers   Cards   Donations

<u>*Received From*</u>   <u>*Item*</u>   <u>*Thanked*</u>

_____ ☐

_____ ☐

_____ ☐

_____ ☐

_____ ☐

_____ ☐

_____ ☐

_____ ☐

_____ ☐

_____ ☐

_____ ☐

_____ ☐

_____ ☐

Gift Log

Flowers Cards Donations

Received From	*Item*	*Thanked*
		☐
		☐
		☐
		☐
		☐
		☐
		☐
		☐
		☐
		☐
		☐
		☐
		☐

Gift Log

Flowers   Cards   Donations

Received From	*Item*	*Thanked*
		☐
		☐
		☐
		☐
		☐
		☐
		☐
		☐
		☐
		☐
		☐
		☐
		☐

Gift Log

Flowers Cards Donations

Received From	*Item*	*Thanked*
		☐
		☐
		☐
		☐
		☐
		☐
		☐
		☐
		☐
		☐
		☐
		☐
		☐

Gift Log

Flowers   Cards   Donations

Received From   *Item*   *Thanked*

_____   ☐

_____   ☐

_____   ☐

_____   ☐

_____   ☐

_____   ☐

_____   ☐

_____   ☐

_____   ☐

_____   ☐

_____   ☐

_____   ☐

_____   ☐

Gift Log

Flowers Cards Donations

Received From	*Item*	*Thanked*
		☐
		☐
		☐
		☐
		☐
		☐
		☐
		☐
		☐
		☐
		☐
		☐
		☐

Gift Log

Flowers   Cards   Donations

Received From	*Item*	*Thanked*
		☐
		☐
		☐
		☐
		☐
		☐
		☐
		☐
		☐
		☐
		☐
		☐
		☐

Gift Log

Flowers Cards Donations

Received From	*Item*	*Thanked*
		☐
		☐
		☐
		☐
		☐
		☐
		☐
		☐
		☐
		☐
		☐
		☐
		☐

Made in the USA
Las Vegas, NV
23 January 2024

84816256R00037